UNIVERSAL GATE CHAPTER
on
AVALOKITESVARA BODHISATTVA

妙法蓮華經觀世音菩薩普門品

Fo Guang Shan International Translation Center

THE LOTUS SUTRA'S UNIVERSAL GATE CHAPTER ON AVALOKITESVARA BODHISATTVA

妙法蓮華經觀世音菩薩普門品

目 錄

Table of Contents

Yang	Zhi	Jing	Shui	Zan
楊	枝	淨	水	讚

Yang	Zhi	Jing	Shui	Bian	Sa	San	Qian
楊	枝	淨	水	遍	灑	三	千

Xing	Kong	Ba	De	Li	Ren	Tian
性	空	八	德	利	人	天

Fu	Shou	Guang	Zeng	Yan
福	壽	廣	增	延

Mie	Zui	Xiao	Qian
滅	罪	消	愆

Huo	Yan	Hua	Hong	Lian
火	燄	化	紅	蓮

Nan	Mo	Guan	Shi	Yin	Pu	Sa
南	無	觀	世	音	菩	薩

Mo	He	Sa	
摩	訶	薩	（三稱）

Praise of Holy Water

With willow twigs, may the holy water be
  sprinkled on the three thousand realms.
May the nature of emptiness and eight virtues
  benefit heaven and earth.
May good fortune and long life both be enhanced
  and extended. May wrongdoing be extinguished and be gone.
Burning flames transform into red lotus blossoms.

We take refuge in Avalokitesvara Bodhisattva-
  Mahasattva. (repeat three times)

Nan Mo Da Bei Guan Shi Yin
南　無　大　悲　觀　世　音

Pu Sa
菩　薩　（三稱）

Kai Jing Ji
　　開　經　偈

Wu Shang Shen Shen Wei Miao Fa
無　上　甚　深　微　妙　法

Bai Qian Wan Jie Nan Zao Yu
百　千　萬　劫　難　遭　遇

Wo Jin Jian Wen De Shou Chi
我　今　見　聞　得　受　持

Yuan Jie Ru Lai Zhen Shi Yi
願　解　如　來　眞　實　義

Homage to great compassionate Avalokitesvara
Bodhisattva.
(repeat three times)

Sutra Opening Verse

The unexcelled, most profound, and exquisitely
  wondrous Dharma,
Is difficult to encounter throughout hundreds of
  thousands of millions of kalpas.
Since we are now able to see, hear, receive and
  retain it,
May we comprehend the true meaning of the
  Tathagata.

妙　法　蓮　華　經

觀　世　音　菩　薩　普　門　品

爾　時　無　盡　意　菩　薩，即

從　座　起，偏　祖　右　肩，合

掌　向　佛，而　作　是　言：「世

尊！觀　世　音　菩　薩　以　何

因　緣　名　觀　世　音？」佛　告

無　盡　意　菩　薩：「善　男　子！

若　有　無　量　百　千　萬　億

6

The Lotus Sutra's Universal Gate Chapter on Avalokitesvara Bodhisattva

At that time, Aksayamati Bodhisattva rose from his seat, bared his right shoulder, put his palms together facing the Buddha, and said, "World-honored One, for what reason is Avalokitesvara Bodhisattva named 'Observing the Sounds of the World'?"

The Buddha answered Aksayamati Bodhisattva, "Good men, if there be countless hundreds of millions of billions of living beings [...]

Zhong	Sheng	Shou	Zhu	Ku	Nao	Wen	Shi
眾	生，	受	諸	苦	惱，	聞	是

Guan	Shi	Yin	Pu	Sa	Yi	Xin	Cheng
觀	世	音	菩	薩，	一	心	稱

Ming	Guan	Shi	Yin	Pu	Sa	Ji	Shi
名，	觀	世	音	菩	薩	即	時

Guan	Qi	Yin	Sheng	Jie	De	Jie	Tuo
觀	其	音	聲，	皆	得	解	脫。

Ruo	You	Chi	Shi	Guan	Shi	Yin	Pu
若	有	持	是	觀	世	音	菩

Sa	Ming	Zhe	She	Ru	Da	Huo	Huo
薩	名	者，	設	入	大	火，	火

Bu	Neng	Shao	You	Shi	Pu	Sa	Wei
不	能	燒，	由	是	菩	薩	威

Shen	Li	Gu	Ruo	Wei	Da	Shui	Suo
神	力	故。	若	爲	大	水	所

Piao	Cheng	Qi	Ming	Hao	Ji	De	Qian
漂，	稱	其	名	號，	即	得	淺

Chu	Ruo	You	Bai	Qian	Wan	Yi	Zhong
處。	若	有	百	千	萬	億	眾

Sheng	Wei	Qiu	Jin	Yin	Liu	Li	Che
生，	爲	求	金、	銀、	琉	璃、	硨

[...] experiencing all manner of suffering who hear of Avalokitesvara Bodhisattva and call his name with single-minded effort, then Avalokitesvara Bodhisattva will instantly observe the sound of their cries, and they will all be liberated.

"If anyone who upholds the name of Avalokitesvara Bodhisattva were to fall into a great fire, the fire would be unable to burn that person due to the bodhisattva's awe-inspiring spiritual powers. If anyone, carried away by a flood, were to call his name, that person would immediately reach a shallow place.

"If there are living beings in the hundreds of millions of billions who go out to sea in search of such treasures as gold, silver, lapis lazuli, mother of pearl,

Qu	Ma	Nao	Shan	Hu	Hu	Po	Zhen
磲、	瑪	瑙、	珊	瑚、	琥	珀、	眞

Zhu	Deng	Bao	Ru	Yu	Da	Hai	Jia
珠	等	寶，	入	於	大	海，	假

Shi	Hei	Feng	Chui	Qi	Chuan	Fang	Piao
使	黑	風	吹	其	船	舫，	漂

Duo	Luo	Cha	Gui	Guo	Qi	Zhong	Ruo
墮	羅	刹	鬼	國，	其	中	若

You	Nai	Zhi	Yi	Ren	Cheng	Guan	Shi
有	乃	至	一	人	稱	觀	世

Yin	Pu	Sa	Ming	Zhe	Shi	Zhu	Ren
音	菩	薩	名	者，	是	諸	人

Deng	Jie	De	Jie	Tuo	Luo	Cha	Zhi
等，	皆	得	解	脫	羅	刹	之

Nan	Yi	Shi	Yin	Yuan	Ming	Guan	Shi
難。	以	是	因	緣，	名	觀	世

Yin	Ruo	Fu	You	Ren	Lin	Dang	Bei
音。	若	復	有	人，	臨	當	被

Hai	Cheng	Guan	Shi	Yin	Pu	Sa	Ming
害，	稱	觀	世	音	菩	薩	名

Zhe	Bi	Suo	Zhi	Dao	Zhang	Xun	Duan
者，	彼	所	執	刀	杖，	尋	段

carnelian, coral, amber, and pearls, and if a fierce storm were to blow their ship off course to make landfall in the territory of raksas, and further if among them there is even one person who calls the name of Avalokitesvara Bodhisattva, then all of those people will be liberated from the torment of the raksas. This is why the bodhisattva is named "Observing the Sounds of the World."

"Or if someone facing imminent attack calls the name of Avalokitesvara Bodhisattva, the knives and clubs held by the attackers will then break into pieces, and that person will attain liberation.

Duan	Huai	Er	De	Jie	Tuo	Ruo	San
段	壞，	而	得	解	脫。	若	三

Qian	Da	Qian	Guo	Tu	Man	Zhong	Ye
千	大	千	國	土，	滿	中	夜

Cha	Luo	Cha	Yu	Lai	Nao	Ren	Wen
叉、	羅	剎，	欲	來	惱	人，	聞

Qi	Cheng	Guan	Shi	Yin	Pu	Sa	Ming
其	稱	觀	世	音	菩	薩	名

Zhe	Shi	Zhu	E	Gui	Shang	Bu	Neng
者，	是	諸	惡	鬼	尚	不	能

Yi	E	Yan	Shi	Zhi	Kuang	Fu	Jia
以	惡	眼	視	之，	況	復	加

Hai	She	Fu	You	Ren	Ruo	You	Zui
害？	設	復	有	人，	若	有	罪、

Ruo	Wu	Zui	Chou	Xie	Jia	Suo	Jian
若	無	罪，	杻	械	枷	鎖	檢

Xi	Qi	Shen	Cheng	Guan	Shi	Yin	Pu
繫	其	身，	稱	觀	世	音	菩

Sa	Ming	Zhe	Jie	Xi	Duan	Huai	Ji
薩	名	者，	皆	悉	斷	壞，	即

De	Jie	Tuo	Ruo	San	Qian	Da	Qian
得	解	脫。	若	三	千	大	千

"If a great three thousand-fold world system was full of yaksas and raksas seeking to torment people, and they heard someone call the name of Avalokitesvara Bodhisattva, these evil demons would not even be able to see that person with their evil eyes, much less do any harm.

"Or if someone, whether guilty or not guilty, who is bound and fettered with manacles, shackles, and cangue calls the name of Avalokitesvara Bodhisattva, then all the bonds will be broken, and that person will instantly attain liberation.

[...]

Guo	Tu	Man	Zhong	Yuan	Zei	You	Yi
國	土，	滿	中	怨	賊，	有	一

Shang	Zhu	Jiang	Zhu	Shang	Ren	Ji	Chi
商	主	將	諸	商	人，	齎	持

Zhong	Bao	Jing	Guo	Xian	Lu	Qi	Zhong
重	寶，	經	過	險	路，	其	中

Yi	Ren	Zuo	Shi	Chang	Yan	Zhu	Shan
一	人	作	是	唱	言：	「諸	善

Nan	Zi	Wu	De	Kong	Bu	Ru	Deng
男	子！	勿	得	恐	怖，	汝	等

Ying	Dang	Yi	Xin	Cheng	Guan	Shi	Yin
應	當	一	心	稱	觀	世	音

Pu	Sa	Ming	Hao	Shi	Pu	Sa	Neng
菩	薩	名	號，	是	菩	薩	能

Yi	Wu	Wei	Shi	Yu	Zhong	Sheng	Ru
以	無	畏	施	於	眾	生；	汝

Deng	Ruo	Cheng	Ming	Zhe	Yu	Ci	Yuan
等	若	稱	名	者，	於	此	怨

Zei	Dang	De	Jie	Tuo	Zhong	Shang	Ren
賊，	當	得	解	脫！」	眾	商	人

Wen	Ju	Fa	Sheng	Yan	Nan	Mo	Guan
聞，	俱	發	聲	言：	「南	無	觀

[...] "If a great three thousand-fold world system were full of malevolent brigands, and a merchant chief were leading many merchants carrying valuable treasures along a perilous road, and among them one man were to speak up and say, "Good men, do not be afraid. You should call the name of Avalokitesvara Bodhisattva with single-minded effort, for this bodhisattva can bestow fearlessness upon living beings. If you call his name, then you will surely be liberated from these malevolent brigands!" [...]

Shi	Yin	Pu	Sa	Cheng	Qi	Ming	Gu
世	音	菩	薩！」	稱	其	名	故，

Ji	De	Jie	Tuo	Wu	Jin	Yi	Guan
即	得	解	脫。	無	盡	意！	觀

Shi	Yin	Pu	Sa	Mo	He	Sa	Wei
世	音	菩	薩	摩	訶	薩	威

Shen	Zhi	Li	Wei	Wei	Ru	Shi	Ruo
神	之	力，	巍	巍	如	是。	若

You	Zhong	Sheng	Duo	Yu	Yin	Yu	Chang
有	眾	生	多	於	淫	欲，	常

Nian	Gong	Jing	Guan	Shi	Yin	Pu	Sa
念	恭	敬	觀	世	音	菩	薩，

Bian	De	Li	Yu	Ruo	Duo	Chen	Hui
便	得	離	欲。	若	多	瞋	恚，

Chang	Nian	Gong	Jing	Guan	Shi	Yin	Pu
常	念	恭	敬	觀	世	音	菩

Sa	Bian	De	Li	Chen	Ruo	Duo	Yu
薩，	便	得	離	瞋。	若	多	愚

Chi	Chang	Nian	Gong	Jing	Guan	Shi	Yin
癡，	常	念	恭	敬	觀	世	音

Pu	Sa	Bian	De	Li	Chi	Wu	Jin
菩	薩，	便	得	離	癡。	無	盡

[...] and upon hearing this, if all of the merchants were to call out: "I take refuge in Avalokitesvara Bodhisattva," then by calling his name, they would instantly attain liberation.

"Aksayamati, lofty indeed are the awe-inspiring spiritual powers of the great Avalokitesvara Bodhisattva.

"If any living beings are much given to greed, let them keep in mind and revere Avalokitesvara Bodhisattva, and they will be freed from their greed.

"If any are much given to anger, let them keep in mind and revere Avalokitesvara Bodhisattva, and they will be freed from their anger.

"If any are much given to ignorance, let them keep in mind and revere Avalokitesvara Bodhisattva, and they will be freed from their ignorance.

[...]

Yi	Guan	Shi	Yin	Pu	Sa	You	Ru
意！	觀	世	音	菩	薩	有	如

Shi	Deng	Da	Wei	Shen	Li	Duo	Suo
是	等	大	威	神	力，	多	所

Rao	Yi	Shi	Gu	Zhong	Sheng	Chang	Ying
饒	益，	是	故	眾	生	常	應

Xin	Nian	Ruo	You	Nü	Ren	She	Yu
心	念。	若	有	女	人，	設	欲

Qiu	Nan	Li	Bai	Gong	Yang	Guan	Shi
求	男，	禮	拜	供	養	觀	世

Yin	Pu	Sa	Bian	Sheng	Fu	De	Zhi
音	菩	薩，	便	生	福	德	智

Hui	Zhi	Nan	She	Yu	Qiu	Nü	Bian
慧	之	男；	設	欲	求	女，	便

Sheng	Duan	Zheng	You	Xiang	Zhi	Nü	Su
生	端	正	有	相	之	女，	宿

Zhi	De	Ben	Zhong	Ren	Ai	Jing	Wu
植	德	本，	眾	人	愛	敬。	無

Jin	Yi	Guan	Shi	Yin	Pu	Sa	You
盡	意！	觀	世	音	菩	薩	有

Ru	Shi	Li	Ruo	You	Zhong	Sheng	Gong
如	是	力。	若	有	眾	生	恭

[...] "Aksayamati, Avalokitesvara Bodhisattva possesses such awe-inspiring spiritual powers, and many have benefited from them. This is why living beings should constantly keep him in mind.

"If any woman wishes for a male child by worshipping and making offerings to Avalokitesvara Bodhisattva, she will then give birth to a son blessed with merit and wisdom. If she wishes for a female child, she will then give birth to a daughter blessed with well-formed and attractive features, one who has planted the roots of virtue over lifetimes and is cherished and respected by all. Aksayamati, such are the powers of Avalokitesvara Bodhisattva!

[...]

Jing	Li	Bai	Guan	Shi	Yin	Pu	Sa
敬	禮	拜	觀	世	音	菩	薩，
Fu	Bu	Tang	Juan	Shi	Gu	Zhong	Sheng
福	不	唐	捐。	是	故	眾	生
Jie	Ying	Shou	Chi	Guan	Shi	Yin	Pu
皆	應	受	持	觀	世	音	菩
Sa	Ming	Hao	Wu	Jin	Yi	Ruo	You
薩	名	號。	無	盡	意！	若	有
Ren	Shou	Chi	Liu	Shi	Er	Yi	Heng
人	受	持	六	十	二	億	恒
He	Sha	Pu	Sa	Ming	Zi	Fu	Jin
河	沙	菩	薩	名	字，	復	盡
Xing	Gong	Yang	Yin	Shi	Yi	Fu	Wo
形	供	養	飲	食、	衣	服、	臥
Ju	Yi	Yao	Yu	Ru	Yi	Yun	He
具、	醫	藥，	於	汝	意	云	何？
Shi	Shan	Nan	Zi	Shan	Nü	Ren	Gong
是	善	男	子、	善	女	人	功
De	Duo	Fou	Wu	Jin	Yi	Yan	Shen
德	多	不？」	無	盡	意	言：	「甚
Duo	Shi	Zun	Fo	Yan	Ruo	Fu	You
多，	世	尊！」	佛	言：	「若	復	有

[...] "If any living being reveres and worships Avalokitesvara Bodhisattva, their auspicious merit will not have been in vain.

"Therefore, let all living beings accept and uphold the name of Avalokitesvara Bodhisattva. Aksayamati, suppose someone were to accept and uphold the names of as many bodhisattvas as there are grains of sand along sixty-two hundred million Ganges Rivers, and spend a lifetime in making offerings of food, drink, clothing, lodging, and medicines to them. What do you think? Would the merit for such a good man or good woman be great or not?"

Aksayamati replied, "Great indeed, World-honored One."

[...]

Ren	Shou	Chi	Guan	Shi	Yin	Pu	Sa
人	受	持	觀	世	音	菩	薩

Ming	Hao	Nai	Zhi	Yi	Shi	Li	Bai
名	號，	乃	至	一	時	禮	拜

Gong	Yang	Shi	Er	Ren	Fu	Zheng	Deng
供	養，	是	二	人	福，	正	等

Wu	Yi	Yu	Bai	Qian	Wan	Yi	Jie
無	異，	於	百	千	萬	億	劫，

Bu	Ke	Qiong	Jin	Wu	Jin	Yi	Shou
不	可	窮	盡。	無	盡	意！	受

Chi	Guan	Shi	Yin	Pu	Sa	Ming	Hao
持	觀	世	音	菩	薩	名	號，

De	Ru	Shi	Wu	Liang	Wu	Bian	Fu
得	如	是	無	量	無	邊	福

De	Zhi	Li	Wu	Jin	Yi	Pu	Sa
德	之	利。」	無	盡	意	菩	薩

Bai	Fo	Yan	Shi	Zun	Guan	Shi	Yin
白	佛	言：「世	尊！	觀	世	音

Pu	Sa	Yun	He	You	Ci	Suo	Po
菩	薩	云	何	遊	此	娑	婆

Shi	Jie	Yun	He	Er	Wei	Zhong	Sheng
世	界？	云	何	而	爲	眾	生

[...] The Buddha said, "Suppose there is another person who accepts and upholds the name of Avalokitesvara Bodhisattva, and worships and makes offerings to him for a single moment; the merit gained by these two people will be exactly the same without any difference. Such merit cannot be exhausted even in hundreds of millions of billions of kalpas. Aksayamati, such are the immeasurable and limitless benefits of the auspicious merit one obtains from accepting and upholding the name of Avalokitesvara Bodhisattva."

Aksayamati Bodhisattva said to the Buddha, "World-honored One, how does Avalokitesvara Bodhisattva wanders through this Saha World? How does he teach the Dharma for the sake of living beings? How does he apply the power of skillful means?"

Shuo	Fa	Fang	Bian	Zhi	Li	Qi	Shi
說	法？	方	便	之	力，	其	事

Yun	He	Fo	Gao	Wu	Jin	Yi	Pu
云	何？」	佛	告	無	盡	意	菩

Sa	Shan	Nan	Zi	Ruo	You	Guo	Tu
薩：	「善	男	子！	若	有	國	土

Zhong	Sheng	Ying	Yi	Fo	Shen	De	Du
眾	生，	應	以	佛	身	得	度

Zhe	Guan	Shi	Yin	Pu	Sa	Ji	Xian
者，	觀	世	音	菩	薩	即	現

Fo	Shen	Er	Wei	Shuo	Fa	Ying	Yi
佛	身	而	爲	說	法。	應	以

Pi	Zhi	Fo	Shen	De	Du	Zhe	Ji
辟	支	佛	身	得	度	者，	即

Xian	Pi	Zhi	Fo	Shen	Er	Wei	Shuo
現	辟	支	佛	身	而	爲	說

Fa	Ying	Yi	Sheng	Wen	Shen	De	Du
法。	應	以	聲	聞	身	得	度

Zhe	Ji	Xian	Sheng	Wen	Shen	Er	Wei
者，	即	現	聲	聞	身	而	爲

Shuo	Fa	Ying	Yi	Fan	Wang	Shen	De
說	法。	應	以	梵	王	身	得

The Buddha told Aksayamati Bodhisattva, "Good men, if there are living beings in this land who should be liberated by someone in the form of a Buddha, then Avalokitesvara Bodhisattva will manifest in the form of a Buddha and teach the Dharma to them."

"For those who should be liberated by someone in the form of a pratyekabuddha, then Avalokitesvara Bodhisattva will manifest in the form of a pratyeka-buddha and teach the Dharma to them. For those who should be liberated by someone in the form of a sravaka, then he will manifest in the form of a sravaka and teach the Dharma to them.

[...]

Du	Zhe	Ji	Xian	Fan	Wang	Shen	Er
度	者，	即	現	梵	王	身	而
Wei	Shuo	Fa	Ying	Yi	Di	Shi	Shen
爲	說	法。	應	以	帝	釋	身
De	Du	Zhe	Ji	Xian	Di	Shi	Shen
得	度	者，	即	現	帝	釋	身
Er	Wei	Shuo	Fa	Ying	Yi	Zi	Zai
而	爲	說	法。	應	以	自	在
Tian	Shen	De	Du	Zhe	Ji	Xian	Zi
天	身	得	度	者，	即	現	自
Zai	Tian	Shen	Er	Wei	Shuo	Fa	Ying
在	天	身	而	爲	說	法。	應
Yi	Da	Zi	Zai	Tian	Shen	De	Du
以	大	自	在	天	身	得	度
Zhe	Ji	Xian	Da	Zi	Zai	Tian	Shen
者，	即	現	大	自	在	天	身
Er	Wei	Shuo	Fa	Ying	Yi	Tian	Da
而	爲	說	法。	應	以	天	大
Jiang	Jun	Shen	De	Du	Zhe	Ji	Xian
將	軍	身	得	度	者，	即	現
Tian	Da	Jiang	Jun	Shen	Er	Wei	Shuo
天	大	將	軍	身	而	爲	說

[...] "For those who should be liberated by someone in the form of King Brahma, then he will manifest in the form of King Brahma and teach the Dharma to them. For those who should be liberated by someone in the form of Lord Sakra, then he will manifest in the form of Lord Sakra and teach the Dharma to them. For those who should be liberated by someone in the form of Isvara, then he will manifest in the form of Isvara and teach the Dharma to them.

"For those who should be liberated by someone in the form of the Mahesvara, then he will manifest in the form of the Mahesvara and teach the Dharma to them. For those who should be liberated by someone in the form of a great heavenly general, then he will manifest in the form of a great heavenly general and teach the Dharma to them. [...]

Fa	Ying	Yi	Pi	Sha	Men	Shen	De
法。	應	以	毗	沙	門	身	得

Du	Zhe	Ji	Xian	Pi	Sha	Men	Shen
度	者，	即	現	毗	沙	門	身

Er	Wei	Shuo	Fa	Ying	Yi	Xiao	Wang
而	爲	說	法。	應	以	小	王

Shen	De	Du	Zhe	Ji	Xian	Xiao	Wang
身	得	度	者，	即	現	小	王

Shen	Er	Wei	Shuo	Fa	Ying	Yi	Zhang
身	而	爲	說	法。	應	以	長

Zhe	Shen	De	Du	Zhe	Ji	Xian	Zhang
者	身	得	度	者，	即	現	長

Zhe	Shen	Er	Wei	Shuo	Fa	Ying	Yi
者	身	而	爲	說	法。	應	以

Ju	Shi	Shen	De	Du	Zhe	Ji	Xian
居	士	身	得	度	者，	即	現

Ju	Shi	Shen	Er	Wei	Shuo	Fa	Ying
居	士	身	而	爲	說	法。	應

Yi	Zai	Guan	Shen	De	Du	Zhe	Ji
以	宰	官	身	得	度	者，	即

Xian	Zai	Guan	Shen	Er	Wei	Shuo	Fa
現	宰	官	身	而	爲	說	法。

[...] For those who should be liberated by someone in the form of Vaisravana, then he will manifest in the form of Vaisravana and teach the Dharma to them.

"For those who should be liberated by someone in the form of a lesser king, then he will manifest in the form of a lesser king and teach the Dharma to them. For those who should be liberated by someone in the form of an elder, then he will manifest in the form of an elder and teach the Dharma to them. For those who should be liberated by someone in the form of a layperson, then he will manifest in the form of a layperson and teach the Dharma to them. For those who should be liberated by someone in the form of a minister, then he will manifest in the form of a minister and teach the Dharma to them. [...]

Ying	Yi	Po	Luo	Men	Shen	De	Du
應	以	婆	羅	門	身	得	度

Zhe	Ji	Xian	Po	Luo	Men	Shen	Er
者，	即	現	婆	羅	門	身	而

Wei	Shuo	Fa	Ying	Yi	Bi	Qiu	Bi
爲	說	法。	應	以	比	丘、	比

Qiu	Ni	You	Po	Se	You	Po	Yi
丘	尼、	優	婆	塞、	優	婆	夷

Shen	De	Du	Zhe	Ji	Xian	Bi	Qiu
身	得	度	者，	即	現	比	丘、

Bi	Qiu	Ni	You	Po	Se	You	Po
比	丘	尼、	優	婆	塞、	優	婆

Yi	Shen	Er	Wei	Shuo	Fa	Ying	Yi
夷	身	而	爲	說	法。	應	以

Zhang	Zhe	Ju	Shi	Zai	Guan	Po	Luo
長	者、	居	士、	宰	官、	婆	羅

Men	Fu	Nü	Shen	De	Du	Zhe	Ji
門	婦	女	身	得	度	者，	即

Xian	Fu	Nü	Shen	Er	Wei	Shuo	Fa
現	婦	女	身	而	爲	說	法。

Ying	Yi	Tong	Nan	Tong	Nü	Shen	De
應	以	童	男	童	女	身	得

[...] For those who should be liberated by someone in the form of a brahman, then he will manifest in the form of a brahman and teach the Dharma to them.

"For those who should be liberated by someone in the form of a bhiksu, a bhiksuni, an upasaka, or an upasika, then he will manifest in the form of a bhiksu, a bhiksuni, an upasaka, or an upasika and teach the Dharma to them.

"For those who should be liberated by someone in the form of a woman from the family of an elder, a lay-person, a minister, or a brahman, then he will manifest in the form of a woman and teach the Dharma to them.

[...]

Du	Zhe	Ji	Xian	Tong	Nan	Tong	Nü
度	者，	即	現	童	男	童	女
Shen	Er	Wei	Shuo	Fa	Ying	Yi	Tian
身	而	爲	說	法。	應	以	天、
Long	Ye	Cha	Qian	Ta	Po	A	Xiu
龍、	夜	叉、	乾	闥	婆、	阿	修
Luo	Jia	Lou	Luo	Jin	Na	Luo	Mo
羅、	迦	樓	羅、	緊	那	羅、	摩
Hou	Luo	Qie	Ren	Fei	Ren	Deng	Shen
睺	羅	伽、	人、	非	人	等	身
De	Du	Zhe	Ji	Jie	Xian	Zhi	Er
得	度	者，	即	皆	現	之	而
Wei	Shuo	Fa	Ying	Yi	Zhi	Jin	Gang
爲	說	法。	應	以	執	金	剛
Shen	De	Du	Zhe	Ji	Xian	Zhi	Jin
神	得	度	者，	即	現	執	金
Gang	Shen	Er	Wei	Shuo	Fa	Wu	Jin
剛	神	而	爲	說	法。	無	盡
Yi	Shi	Guan	Shi	Yin	Pu	Sa	Cheng
意！	是	觀	世	音	菩	薩，	成
Jiu	Ru	Shi	Gong	De	Yi	Zhong	Zhong
就	如	是	功	德。	以	種	種

[...] "For those who should be liberated by someone in the form of a young boy or young girl, then he will manifest in the form of a young boy or young girl and teach the Dharma to them.

"For those who should be liberated by someone in such forms as a deva, a naga, a yaksa, a gandharva, an asura, a garuda, a kimnara, a mahoraga, a human or a nonhuman being, then he will manifest in all these forms and teach the Dharma to them.

"For those who should be liberated by a vajrapani deity, then he will manifest as a vajrapani deity and teach the Dharma to them.

"Aksayamati, such is the merit that Avalokitesvara Bodhisattva has accomplished, and the various forms in which he wanders the various lands bringing liberation to living beings.

Xing 形，You 遊 Zhu 諸 Guo 國 Tu 土，Du 度 Tuo 脫 Zhong 眾

Sheng 生。Shi 是 Gu 故 Ru 汝 Deng 等 Ying 應 Dang 當 Yi 一

Xin 心 Gong 供 Yang 養 Guan 觀 Shi 世 Yin 音 Pu 菩 Sa 薩。

Shi 是 Guan 觀 Shi 世 Yin 音 Pu 菩 Sa 薩 Mo 摩 He 訶

Sa 薩，Yu 於 Bu 怖 Wei 畏 Ji 急 Nan 難 Zhi 之 Zhong 中，

Neng 能 Shi 施 Wu 無 Wei 畏，Shi 是 Gu 故 Ci 此 Suo 娑

Po 婆 Shi 世 Jie 界，Jie 皆 Hao 號 Zhi 之 Wei 爲 Shi 施

Wu 無 Wei 畏 Zhe 者。」Wu 無 Jin 盡 Yi 意 Pu 菩 Sa 薩

Bai 白 Fo 佛 Yan 言：Shi 「世 Zun 尊！Wo 我 Jin 今 Dang 當

Gong 供 Yang 養 Guan 觀 Shi 世 Yin 音 Pu 菩 Sa 薩。」Ji 即

Jie 解 Jing 頸 Zhong 眾 Bao 寶 Zhu 珠 Ying 瓔 Luo 珞，Jia 價

"This is why all of you should single-mindedly make offerings to Avalokitesvara Bodhisattva, for it is the great Avalokitesvara Bodhisattva who can bestow fearlessness in the midst of terror and in dire circumstances. This is why everyone in this Saha World calls him the bestower of fearlessness."

Aksayamati Bodhisattva said to the Buddha, "World-honored One, now I must make an offering to Avalokitesvara Bodhisattva." [...]

Zhi	Bai	Qian	Liang	Jin	Er	Yi	Yu
值	百	千	兩	金，	而	以	與

Zhi	Zuo	Shi	Yan	Ren	Zhe	Shou	Ci
之。	作	是	言：	「仁	者！	受	此

Fa	Shi	Zhen	Bao	Ying	Luo	Shi	Guan
法	施，	珍	寶	瓔	珞。」	時	觀

Shi	Yin	Pu	Sa	Bu	Ken	Shou	Zhi
世	音	菩	薩	不	肯	受	之。

Wu	Jin	Yi	Fu	Bai	Guan	Shi	Yin
無	盡	意	復	白	觀	世	音

Pu	Sa	Yan	Ren	Zhe	Min	Wo	Deng
菩	薩	言：	「仁	者！	愍	我	等

Gu	Shou	Ci	Ying	Luo	Er	Shi	Fo
故，	受	此	瓔	珞。」	爾	時	佛

Gao	Guan	Shi	Yin	Pu	Sa	Dang	Min
告	觀	世	音	菩	薩：	「當	愍

Ci	Wu	Jin	Yi	Pu	Sa	Ji	Si
此	無	盡	意	菩	薩，	及	四

Zhong	Tian	Long	Ye	Cha	Qian	Ta	Po
眾、	天、	龍、	夜	叉、	乾	闥	婆、

A	Xiu	Luo	Jia	Lou	Luo	Jin	Na
阿	修	羅、	迦	樓	羅、	緊	那

[...] Then he took from his neck a necklace of numerous precious gems worth thousands of ounces in gold, and gave it to him saying, "Kind one, accept this necklace of precious gems as a Dharma gift."

At the time, Avalokitesvara Bodhisattva was unwilling to accept it. Aksayamati spoke once more to Avalokitesvara Bodhisattva, "Kind one, accept this necklace as a kindness to us."

Then the Buddha said to Avalokitesvara Bodhisattva, "Accept this jeweled necklace out of compassion for Aksayamati Bodhisattva, as well as the four groups of Buddhist disciples, the devas, nagas, yaksas, gandharvas, asuras, garudas, kimnaras, mahoragas, human and nonhuman beings." [...]

Luo	Mo	Hou	Luo	Qie	Ren	Fei	Ren
羅、	摩	睺	羅	伽、	人、	非	人
Deng	Gu	Shou	Shi	Ying	Luo	Ji	Shi
等	故，	受	是	瓔	珞。」	即	時
Guan	Shi	Yin	Pu	Sa	Min	Zhu	Si
觀	世	音	菩	薩，	愍	諸	四
Zhong	Ji	Yu	Tian	Long	Ren	Fei	Ren
眾，	及	於	天、	龍、	人、	非	人
Deng	Shou	Qi	Ying	Luo	Fen	Zuo	Er
等，	受	其	瓔	珞，	分	作	二
Fen	Yi	Fen	Feng	Shi	Jia	Mou	Ni
分：	一	分	奉	釋	迦	牟	尼
Fo	Yi	Fen	Feng	Duo	Bao	Fo	Ta
佛，	一	分	奉	多	寶	佛	塔。
Wu	Jin	Yi	Guan	Shi	Yin	Pu	Sa
「無	盡	意！	觀	世	音	菩	薩，
You	Ru	Shi	Zi	Zai	Shen	Li	You
有	如	是	自	在	神	力，	遊
Yu	Suo	Po	Shi	Jie	Er	Shi	Wu
於	娑	婆	世	界。」	爾	時	無
Jin	Yi	Pu	Sa	Yi	Ji	Wen	Yue
盡	意	菩	薩	以	偈	問	曰：

[...] Thereupon, Avalokitesvara Bodhisattva accepted the jeweled necklace out of compassion for the four groups of Buddhist disciples, the devas and nagas, and the human and nonhuman beings, and dividing it into two parts, presented one part to Sakyamuni Buddha and presented the other part to the stupa of Prabhuta-ratna Buddha.

"Aksayamati, it is with such freely exercised spiritual powers that Avalokitesvara Bodhisattva wanders through the Saha World."

Then Aksayamati Bodhisattva asked his question in verse:

Shi	Zun	Miao	Xiang	Ju
世	尊	妙	相	具，

Wo	Jin	Chong	Wen	Bi
我	今	重	問	彼：

Fo	Zi	He	Yin	Yuan
佛	子	何	因	緣，

Ming	Wei	Guan	Shi	Yin
名	爲	觀	世	音？

Ju	Zu	Miao	Xiang	Zun
具	足	妙	相	尊，

Ji	Da	Wu	Jin	Yi
偈	答	無	盡	意：

Ru	Ting	Guan	Yin	Xing
汝	聽	觀	音	行，

Shan	Ying	Zhu	Fang	Suo
善	應	諸	方	所，

Hong	Shi	Shen	Ru	Hai
弘	誓	深	如	海，

Li	Jie	Bu	Si	Yi
歷	劫	不	思	議，

Shi	Duo	Qian	Yi	Fo
侍	多	千	億	佛，

"World-honored One with all the wonderful signs,

Let me now ask about him once more:

For what reason is this son of the Buddha

Named 'Observing the Sounds of the World'?"

World-honored One with all the wonderful signs

Answered Aksayamati in verse:

"You listen now to the practice of Avalokitesvara,

Who well responds to every region.

His great vow is as deep as the sea,

Inconceivable even after many kalpas.

Having served Buddhas in the hundreds of billions,

Fa	Da	Qing	Jing	Yuan
發	大	清	淨	願。

Wo	Wei	Ru	Lüe	Shuo
我	爲	汝	略	說,

Wen	Ming	Ji	Jian	Shen
聞	名	及	見	身,

Xin	Nian	Bu	Kong	Guo
心	念	不	空	過,

Neng	Mie	Zhu	You	Ku
能	滅	諸	有	苦。

Jia	Shi	Xing	Hai	Yi
假	使	興	害	意,

Tui	Luo	Da	Huo	Keng
推	落	大	火	坑,

Nian	Bi	Guan	Yin	Li
念	彼	觀	音	力,

Huo	Keng	Bian	Cheng	Chi
火	坑	變	成	池。

Huo	Piao	Liu	Ju	Hai
或	漂	流	巨	海,

Long	Yu	Zhu	Gui	Nan
龍	魚	諸	鬼	難,

He has made a great and pure vow.

Let me briefly tell you:

Hearing his name and seeing his form,

Keeping him unremittingly in mind,

Can eliminate all manner of suffering.

Suppose someone with harmful intent,

Casts you into a great pit of fire;

Keep in mind Avalokitesvara's powers,

And the pit of fire will change into a pond.

Or you are cast adrift upon an immense ocean,

Menaced by dragons, fish, and demons;

Nian Bi Guan Yin Li
念 彼 觀 音 力，

Bo Lang Bu Neng Mo
波 浪 不 能 沒。

Huo Zai Xu Mi Feng
或 在 須 彌 峰，

Wei Ren Suo Tui Duo
爲 人 所 推 墮，

Nian Bi Guan Yin Li
念 彼 觀 音 力，

Ru Ri Xu Kong Zhu
如 日 虛 空 住。

Huo Bei E Ren Zhu
或 被 惡 人 逐，

Duo Luo Jin Gang Shan
墮 落 金 剛 山，

Nian Bi Guan Yin Li
念 彼 觀 音 力，

Bu Neng Sun Yi Mao
不 能 損 一 毛。

Huo Zhi Yuan Zei Rao
或 值 怨 賊 繞，

Keep in mind Avalokitesvara's powers,

And the waves will not drown you.

Or someone pushes you down,

From the top of Mount Sumeru;

Keep in mind Avalokitesvara's powers,

And you will hang in the sky like the sun.

Or you are pursued by evil doers,

Who push you down from Mount Vajra;

Keep in mind Avalokitesvara's powers,

And not one of your hairs will be harmed.

Or if surrounded by malevolent brigands,

Ge	Zhi	Dao	Jia	Hai
各	執	刀	加	害，

Nian	Bi	Guan	Yin	Li
念	彼	觀	音	力，

Xian	Ji	Qi	Ci	Xin
咸	即	起	慈	心。

Huo	Zao	Wang	Nan	Ku
或	遭	王	難	苦，

Lin	Xing	Yu	Shou	Zhong
臨	刑	欲	壽	終，

Nian	Bi	Guan	Yin	Li
念	彼	觀	音	力，

Dao	Xun	Duan	Duan	Huai
刀	尋	段	段	壞。

Huo	Qiu	Jin	Jia	Suo
或	囚	禁	枷	鎖，

Shou	Zu	Bei	Chou	Xie
手	足	被	杻	械，

Nian	Bi	Guan	Yin	Li
念	彼	觀	音	力，

Shi	Ran	De	Jie	Tuo
釋	然	得	解	脫。

Each one brandishing a knife to attack you;

Keep in mind Avalokitesvara's powers,

And they will all experience a sense of compassion.

Or if persecuted by the royal court,

Facing death by execution;

Keep in mind Avalokitesvara's powers,

And the executioner's blade will break into pieces.

Or if imprisoned with cangue and chains,

Hands and feet manacled and shackled;

Keep in mind Avalokitesvara's powers,

And the bonds will loosen and you will be liberated.

Zhou	Zu	Zhu	Du	Yao
咒	詛	諸	毒	藥，
Suo	Yu	Hai	Shen	Zhe
所	欲	害	身	者，
Nian	Bi	Guan	Yin	Li
念	彼	觀	音	力，
Huan	Zhuo	Yu	Ben	Ren
還	著	於	本	人。
Huo	Yu	E	Luo	Cha
或	遇	惡	羅	剎，
Du	Long	Zhu	Gui	Deng
毒	龍	諸	鬼	等，
Nian	Bi	Guan	Yin	Li
念	彼	觀	音	力，
Shi	Xi	Bu	Gan	Hai
時	悉	不	敢	害。
Ruo	E	Shou	Wei	Rao
若	惡	獸	圍	繞，
Li	Ya	Zhao	Ke	Bu
利	牙	爪	可	怖，
Nian	Bi	Guan	Yin	Li
念	彼	觀	音	力，

If there is someone who would do you harm,

Using spells and various poisons;

Keep in mind Avalokitesvara's powers,

And any harm will rebound on the originator.

Or if you encounter evil raksas,

Venomous dragons, various ghosts, and the like;

Keep in mind Avalokitesvara's powers,

And then none of them will dare harm you.

If you are surrounded by evil beasts

With their sharp teeth and claws so horrifying;

Keep in mind Avalokitesvara's powers,

Ji	Zou	Wu	Bian	Fang
疾	走	無	邊	方。

Yuan	She	Ji	Fu	Xie
蚖	蛇	及	蝮	蠍，

Qi	Du	Yan	Huo	Ran
氣	毒	煙	火	然，

Nian	Bi	Guan	Yin	Li
念	彼	觀	音	力，

Xun	Sheng	Zi	Hui	Qu
尋	聲	自	迴	去。

Yun	Lei	Gu	Che	Dian
雲	雷	鼓	掣	電，

Jiang	Bao	Shu	Da	Yu
降	雹	澍	大	雨，

Nian	Bi	Guan	Yin	Li
念	彼	觀	音	力，

Ying	Shi	De	Xiao	San
應	時	得	消	散。

Zhong	Sheng	Bei	Kun	E
眾	生	被	困	厄，

Wu	Liang	Ku	Bi	Shen
無	量	苦	逼	身，

And they will flee in all directions.

When lizards, snakes, vipers, and scorpions

Scorch you with their poisonous vapors;

Keep in mind Avalokitesvara's powers,

And they will retreat at the sound of your voice.

When thunderclouds rumble with lighting strikes,

As hailstones and torrential rains come down;

Keep in mind Avalokitesvara's powers,

And the storm will disperse that very moment.

Living beings suffer in agony,

Oppressed by immeasurable pain;

Guan	Yin	Miao	Zhi	Li
觀	音	妙	智	力，

Neng	Jiu	Shi	Jian	Ku
能	救	世	間	苦。

Ju	Zu	Shen	Tong	Li
具	足	神	通	力，

Guang	Xiu	Zhi	Fang	Bian
廣	修	智	方	便，

Shi	Fang	Zhu	Guo	Tu
十	方	諸	國	土，

Wu	Cha	Bu	Xian	Shen
無	剎	不	現	身。

Zhong	Zhong	Zhu	E	Qu
種	種	諸	惡	趣，

Di	Yu	Gui	Chu	Sheng
地	獄	鬼	畜	生，

Sheng	Lao	Bing	Si	Ku
生	老	病	死	苦，

Yi	Jian	Xi	Ling	Mie
以	漸	悉	令	滅。

Zhen	Guan	Qing	Jing	Guan
眞	觀	清	淨	觀，

The power of Avalokitesvara's wondrous wisdom

Can bring liberation from the world's sufferings.

Perfect in supernatural powers,

Widely practicing the skillful means of wisdom,

In all the lands of the ten directions,

There is no place where he fails to manifest.

The lower realms in all their forms,

That of hell-beings, hungry ghosts, and animals,

The sufferings of birth, old age, sickness, and death,

He steadily brings them all to an end.

Contemplation of truth, contemplation of purity,

Guang	Da	Zhi	Hui	Guan
廣	大	智	慧	觀，
Bei	Guan	Ji	Ci	Guan
悲	觀	及	慈	觀，
Chang	Yuan	Chang	Zhan	Yang
常	願	常	瞻	仰。
Wu	Gou	Qing	Jing	Guang
無	垢	清	淨	光，
Hui	Ri	Po	Zhu	An
慧	日	破	諸	闇，
Neng	Fu	Zai	Feng	Huo
能	伏	災	風	火，
Pu	Ming	Zhao	Shi	Jian
普	明	照	世	間。
Bei	Ti	Jie	Lei	Zhen
悲	體	戒	雷	震，
Ci	Yi	Miao	Da	Yun
慈	意	妙	大	雲，
Shu	Gan	Lu	Fa	Yu
澍	甘	露	法	雨，
Mie	Chu	Fan	Nao	Yan
滅	除	煩	惱	燄。

Contemplation of the vast and greater wisdom,

Contemplation of compassion and contemplation
of kindness;

Ever longed for, ever looked up to.

His undefiled light of purity

Is the wisdom-sun dispelling all darkness,

What can quell winds and fires that bring disaster

And illuminate the world universally.

Precepts of his compassionate body are like rolling
thunder;

The profundity of his kind mind is like a great cloud;

He showers us with Dharma rain like nectar,

That extinguishes the flames of affliction.

Zheng	Song	Jing	Guan	Chu
諍	訟	經	官	處，
Bu	Wei	Jun	Zhen	Zhong
怖	畏	軍	陣	中，
Nian	Bi	Guan	Yin	Li
念	彼	觀	音	力，
Zhong	Yuan	Xi	Tui	San
眾	怨	悉	退	散。
Miao	Yin	Guan	Shi	Yin
妙	音	觀	世	音，
Fan	Yin	Hai	Chao	Yin
梵	音	海	潮	音，
Sheng	Bi	Shi	Jian	Yin
勝	彼	世	間	音，
Shi	Gu	Xu	Chang	Nian
是	故	須	常	念。
Nian	Nian	Wu	Sheng	Yi
念	念	勿	生	疑，
Guan	Shi	Yin	Jing	Sheng
觀	世	音	淨	聖，
Yu	Ku	Nao	Si	E
於	苦	惱	死	厄，

When lawsuits bring you to court,

Or when fear strikes you in battle,

Keep in mind Avalokitesvara's powers,

And the enemy forces will all retreat.

Contemplating the world's voices with a wondrous
voice,

A Brahma voice, an ocean-tide voice,

What surpasses those voices of the world;

Therefore constantly keep them in mind.

Never doubt from moment to moment,

The pure and noble Avalokitesvara;

For those in pain and agony, or facing death,

Neng	Wei	Zuo	Yi	Hu
能	爲	作	依	怙。

Ju	Yi	Qie	Gong	De
具	一	切	功	德,

Ci	Yan	Shi	Zhong	Sheng
慈	眼	視	眾	生,

Fu	Ju	Hai	Wu	Liang
福	聚	海	無	量,

Shi	Gu	Ying	Ding	Li
是	故	應	頂	禮。

Er	Shi	Chi	Di	Pu	Sa	Ji	Cong
爾	時	持	地	菩	薩	即	從

Zuo	Qi	Qian	Bai	Fo	Yan	Shi	Zun
座	起,	前	白	佛	言：「世	尊!

Ruo	You	Zhong	Sheng	Wen	Shi	Guan	Shi
若	有	眾	生	聞	是	觀	世

Yin	Pu	Sa	Pin	Zi	Zai	Zhi	Ye
音	菩	薩	品,	自	在	之	業,

Pu	Men	Shi	Xian	Shen	Tong	Li	Zhe
普	門	示	現	神	通	力	者,

Dang	Zhi	Shi	Ren	Gong	De	Bu	Shao
當	知	是	人,	功	德	不	少。」

He can be their aid and support!

In possession of all merit and virtue,

He views living beings with compassionate eyes;

His ocean of accumulated merit is infinite,

So worship him with prostrations.

At this time Dharanimdhara Bodhisattva rose from his seat, came forward, and said to the Buddha, "World-honored One, if there are living beings who hear this chapter on Avalokitesvara Bodhisattva about his freedom of action, his revelation of the universal gate, and his supernatural powers, it should be known that their merits are not few."

[...]

Fo	Shuo	Shi	Pu	Men	Pin	Shi	Zhong
佛	說	是	普	門	品	時，	眾

Zhong	Ba	Wan	Si	Qian	Zhong	Sheng	Jie
中	八	萬	四	千	眾	生	皆

Fa	Wu	Deng	Deng	A	Nou	Duo	Luo
發	無	等	等	阿	耨	多	羅

San	Miao	San	Pu	Ti	Xin
三	藐	三	菩	提	心。

[...] When the Buddha preached this chapter on the Universal Gate, the eighty-four thousand living beings assembled there all generated the aspiration to attain anuttara-samyak-sambodhi.

Bo	Re	Bo	Luo	Mi	Duo	Xin	Jing
般	若	波	羅	蜜	多	心	經

Guan	Zi	Zai	Pu	Sa	Xing	Shen	Bo
觀	自	在	菩	薩，	行	深	般

Re	Bo	Luo	Mi	Duo	Shi	Zhao	Jian
若	波	羅	蜜	多	時，	照	見

Wu	Yun	Jie	Kong	Du	Yi	Qie	Ku
五	蘊	皆	空，	度	一	切	苦

E	She	Li	Zi	Se	Bu	Yi	Kong
厄。	舍	利	子，	色	不	異	空，

Kong	Bu	Yi	Se	Se	Ji	Shi	Kong
空	不	異	色，	色	即	是	空，

Kong	Ji	Shi	Se	Shou	Xiang	Xing	Shi
空	即	是	色，	受	想	行	識，

Yi	Fu	Ru	Shi	She	Li	Zi	Shi
亦	復	如	是。	舍	利	子，	是

Heart Sutra

Avalokitesvara Bodhisattva, while contemplating deeply the prajnaparamita, realized the five aggregates are empty and was liberated from all suffering and hardship.

Sariputra, form is not different from emptiness, emptiness is not different from form. Form is emptiness. Emptiness is form. The same is true of feeling, perception, mental formations, and consciousness.

[...]

Zhu	Fa	Kong	Xiang	Bu	Sheng	Bu	Mie
諸	法	空	相，	不	生	不	滅，
Bu	Gou	Bu	Jing	Bu	Zeng	Bu	Jian
不	垢	不	淨，	不	增	不	減。
Shi	Gu	Kong	Zhong	Wu	Se	Wu	Shou
是	故	空	中	無	色，	無	受
Xiang	Xing	Shi	Wu	Yan	Er	Bi	She
想	行	識。	無	眼	耳	鼻	舌
Shen	Yi	Wu	Se	Sheng	Xiang	Wei	Chu
身	意，	無	色	聲	香	味	觸
Fa	Wu	Yan	Jie	Nai	Zhi	Wu	Yi
法。	無	眼	界，	乃	至	無	意
Shi	Jie	Wu	Wu	Ming	Yi	Wu	Wu
識	界。	無	無	明，	亦	無	無
Ming	Jin	Nai	Zhi	Wu	Lao	Si	Yi
明	盡，	乃	至	無	老	死，	亦
Wu	Lao	Si	Jin	Wu	Ku	Ji	Mie
無	老	死	盡。	無	苦	集	滅
Dao	Wu	Zhi	Yi	Wu	De	Yi	Wu
道，	無	智	亦	無	得。	以	無
Suo	De	Gu	Pu	Ti	Sa	Duo	Yi
所	得	故，	菩	提	薩	埵，	依

[...] Sariputra, all phenomena are empty. They do not arise or cease, are not defiled or pure, do not increase or decrease. Thus, in emptiness, there are no forms, feelings, perceptions, mental formations, or consciousness.

No eye, ear, nose, tongue, body, or mind; no form, sound, smell, taste, touch or dharmas; no eye consciousness so on unto mind consciousness; no ignorance and extinction of ignorance; even unto no aging and death and no extinction of aging and death; no suffering, cause of suffering, cessation, or path; no wisdom and no attainment.

[...]

Bo 般	Re 若	Bo 波	Luo 羅	Mi 蜜	Duo 多	Gu 故，	Xin 心
Wu 無	Gua 罣	Ai 礙，	Wu 無	Gua 罣	Ai 礙	Gu 故，	Wu 無
You 有	Kong 恐	Bu 怖，	Yuan 遠	Li 離	Dian 顛	Dao 倒	Meng 夢
Xiang 想，	Jiu 究	Jing 竟	Nie 涅	Pan 槃。	San 三	Shi 世	Zhu 諸
Fo 佛，	Yi 依	Bo 般	Re 若	Bo 波	Luo 羅	Mi 蜜	Duo 多
Gu 故，	De 得	A 阿	Nou 耨	Duo 多	Luo 羅	San 三	Miao 藐
San 三	Pu 菩	Ti 提。	Gu 故	Zhi 知	Bo 般	Re 若	Bo 波
Luo 羅	Mi 蜜	Duo 多，	Shi 是	Da 大	Shen 神	Zhou 咒，	Shi 是
Da 大	Ming 明	Zhou 咒，	Shi 是	Wu 無	Shang 上	Zhou 咒，	Shi 是
Wu 無	Deng 等	Deng 等	Zhou 咒，	Neng 能	Chu 除	Yi 一	Qie 切
Ku 苦，	Zhen 眞	Shi 實	Bu 不	Xu 虛。	Gu 故	Shuo 說	Bo 般

[...] As there is no attainment, bodhisattvas who rely on the prajnaparamita have neither worry nor obstruction. Without worry and obstruction, there is no fear. Away from confusion and delusion, they will ultimately reach nirvana. All the Buddhas of the past, present, and future rely on the prajnaparamita to attain anuttara-samyak-sambodhi.

Thus, know that the prajnaparamita is the great profound mantra, is the illuminating mantra, is the most supreme of all mantras, is the unequalled mantra, able to eliminate all suffering, is true and not false.

[...]

Re	Bo	Luo	Mi	Duo	Zhou	Ji	Shuo
若	波	羅	蜜	多	咒，	即	說

Zhou	Yue
咒	曰：

Jie	Di	Jie	Di	Bo	Luo	Jie	Di
揭	諦	揭	諦	波	羅	揭	諦

Bo	Luo	Seng	Jie	Di	Pu	Ti	Sa
波	羅	僧	揭	諦	菩	提	薩

Po	He
婆	訶

[...] Thus, proclaim the "Prajnaparamita Mantra," proclaim the mantra that says:

Gate gate paragate parasamgate bodhi svaha.

Qian	Shou	Qian	Yan	Wu	Ai
千	手	千	眼	無	礙

Da	Bei	Xin	Tuo	Luo	Ni
大	悲	心	陀	羅	尼

Nan	Mo	He	La	Da	Na	Duo	La
南	無	喝	囉	怛	那	哆	囉
Ye	Ye	Nan	Mo	A	Li	Ye	Po
夜	耶。	南	無	阿	唎	耶。	婆
Lu	Jie	Di	Shuo	Bo	La	Ye	Pu
盧	羯	帝。	爍	缽	囉	耶。	菩
Ti	Sa	Duo	Po	Ye	Mo	He	Sa
提	薩	埵	婆	耶。	摩	訶	薩
Duo	Po	Ye	Mo	He	Jia	Lu	Ni
埵	婆	耶。	摩	訶	迦	盧	尼
Jia	Ye	An	Sa	Po	La	Fa	Yi
迦	耶。	唵。	薩	皤	囉	罰	曳。

Shu	Da	Na	Da	Xie	Nan	Mo	Xi
數	怛	那	怛	寫。	南	無	悉

Ji	Li	Duo	Yi	Meng	A	Li	Ye
吉	喋	埵	伊	蒙	阿	唎	耶。

Po	Lu	Ji	Di	Shi	Fo	La	Leng
婆	盧	吉	帝，	室	佛	囉	楞

Tuo	Po	Nan	Mo	Na	La	Jin	Chi
馱	婆。	南	無	那	囉	謹	墀。

Xi	Li	Mo	He	Po	Duo	Sha	Mie
醯	利	摩	訶，	皤	哆	沙	咩。

Sa	Po	A	Ta	Dou	Shu	Peng	A
薩	婆	阿	他、	豆	輸	朋。	阿

Shi	Yun	Sa	Po	Sa	Duo	Na	Mo
逝	孕。	薩	婆	薩	哆、	那	摩

Po	Sa	Duo	Na	Mo	Po	Qie	Mo
婆	薩	哆、	那	摩	婆	伽。	摩

Fa	Te	Dou	Da	Zhi	Ta	An	A
罰	特	豆。	怛	姪	他。	唵。	阿

Po	Lu	Xi	Lu	Jia	Di	Jia	Luo
婆	盧	醯。	盧	迦	帝。	迦	羅

Di	Yi	Xi	Li	Mo	He	Pu	Ti
帝。	夷	醯。	唎。	摩	訶	菩	提

Sa	Duo	Sa	Po	Sa	Po	Mo	La
薩	埵。	薩	婆	薩	婆。	摩	囉

Mo	La	Mo	Xi	Mo	Xi	Li	Tuo
摩	囉。	摩	醯	摩	醯。	唎	馱

Yun	Ju	Lu	Ju	Lu	Jie	Meng	Du
孕。	俱	盧	俱	盧	羯	蒙。	度

Lu	Du	Lu	Fa	She	Ye	Di	Mo
盧	度	盧	罰	闍	耶	帝。	摩

He	Fa	She	Ye	Di	Tuo	La	Tuo
訶	罰	闍	耶	帝。	陀	囉	陀

La	Di	Li	Ni	Shi	Fo	La	Ye
囉。	地	唎	尼。	室	佛	囉	耶。

Zhe	La	Zhe	La	Mo	Mo	Fa	Mo
遮	囉	遮	囉。	摩	麼	罰	摩

La	Mu	Di	Li	Yi	Xi	Yi	Xi
囉。	穆	帝	隸。	伊	醯	伊	醯。

Shi	Na	Shi	Na	A	La	San	Fo
室	那	室	那。	阿	囉	嘇	佛

La	She	Li	Fa	Sha	Fa	San	Fo
囉	舍	利。	罰	沙	罰	嘇。	佛

La	She	Ye	Hu	Lu	Hu	Lu	Mo
囉	舍	耶。	呼	嚧	呼	嚧	摩

La	Hu	Lu	Hu	Lu	Xi	Li	Suo
囉。	呼	嚧	呼	嚧	醯	利。	娑

La	Suo	La	Xi	Li	Xi	Li	Su
囉	娑	囉。	悉	唎	悉	唎。	蘇

Lu	Su	Lu	Pu	Ti	Ye	Pu	Ti
嚧	蘇	嚧。	菩	提	夜	菩	提

Ye	Pu	Tuo	Ye	Pu	Tuo	Ye	Mi
夜。	菩	馱	夜	菩	馱	夜。	彌

Di	Li	Ye	Na	La	Jin	Chi	Di
帝	唎	夜。	那	囉	謹	墀。	地

Li	Se	Ni	Na	Po	Ye	Mo	Na
利	瑟	尼	那。	婆	夜	摩	那。

Suo	Po	He	Xi	Tuo	Ye	Suo	Po
娑	婆	訶。	悉	陀	夜。	娑	婆

He	Mo	He	Xi	Tuo	Ye	Suo	Po
訶。	摩	訶	悉	陀	夜。	娑	婆

He	Xi	Tuo	Yu	Yi	Shi	Po	La
訶。	悉	陀	喻	藝。	室	皤	囉

Ye	Suo	Po	He	Na	La	Jin	Chi
耶。	娑	婆	訶。	那	囉	謹	墀。

Suo	Po	He	Mo	La	Na	La	Suo
娑	婆	訶。	摩	囉	那	囉。	娑

Po	He	Xi	La	Seng	A	Mu	Qia
婆	訶。	悉	囉	僧	阿	穆	佉

Ye	Suo	Po	He	Suo	Po	Mo	He
耶。	娑	婆	訶。	娑	婆	摩	訶、

A	Xi	Tuo	Ye	Suo	Po	He	Zhe
阿	悉	陀	夜。	娑	婆	訶。	者

Ji	La	A	Xi	Tuo	Ye	Suo	Po
吉	囉	阿	悉	陀	夜。	娑	婆

He	Po	Tuo	Mo	Jie	Xi	Tuo	Ye
訶。	波	陀	摩	羯	悉	陀	夜。

Suo	Po	He	Na	La	Jin	Chi	Po
娑	婆	訶。	那	囉	謹	墀	皤

Qie	La	Ye	Suo	Po	He	Mo	Po
伽	囉	耶。	娑	婆	訶。	摩	婆

Li	Sheng	Jie	La	Ye	Suo	Po	He
利	勝	羯	囉	夜。	娑	婆	訶。

Nan	Mo	He	La	Da	Na	Duo	La
南	無	喝	囉	怛	那	哆	囉

Ye	Ye	Nan	Mo	A	Li	Ye	Po
夜	耶。	南	無	阿	唎	耶。	婆

Lu	Ji	Di	Shuo	Po	La	Ye	Suo
嚧	吉	帝。	爍	皤	囉	夜。	娑

Po	He	An	Xi	Dian	Du	Man	Duo
婆	訶。	唵。	悉	殿	都。	漫	哆

La	Ba	Tuo	Ye	Suo	Po	He
囉。	跋	陀	耶。	娑	婆	訶。

San Gui Yi
三　皈　依

Zi　Gui　Yi　Fo　Dang　Yuan　Zhong　Sheng
自　皈　依　佛，當　願　眾　生，

Ti　Jie　Da　Dao　Fa　Wu　Shang　Xin
體　解　大　道，發　無　上　心。

Zi　Gui　Yi　Fa　Dang　Yuan　Zhong　Sheng
自　皈　依　法，當　願　眾　生，

Shen　Ru　Jing　Zang　Zhi　Hui　Ru　Hai
深　入　經　藏，智　慧　如　海。

Zi　Gui　Yi　Seng　Dang　Yuan　Zhong　Sheng
自　皈　依　僧，當　願　眾　生，

Tong　Li　Da　Zhong　Yi　Qie　Wu　Ai
統　理　大　眾，一　切　無　礙。

Triple Refuge

I take refuge in the Buddha, wishing that all sentient beings understand the Dharma and make the supreme vow.

I take refuge in the Dharma, wishing that all sentient beings study the sutras diligently and obtain an ocean of wisdom.

I take refuge in the Sangha, wishing that all sentient beings lead the masses in harmony without obstruction.

Hui Xiang Ji
回 向 偈

Ci　Bei　Xi　She　Bian　Fa　Jie
慈　悲　喜　捨　遍　法　界，

Xi　Fu　Jie　Yuan　Li　Ren　Tian
惜　福　結　緣　利　人　天；

Chan　Jing　Jie　Hen　Ping　Deng　Ren
禪　淨　戒　行　平　等　忍，

Can　Kui　Gan　En　Da　Yuan　Xin
慚　愧　感　恩　大　願　心。

Dedication of Merit

May kindness, compassion, joy , and equanimity
   pervade the dharma realms;
May all people and heavenly beings benefit from
   our blessings and friendship;
May our ethical practice of Chan, Pure Land, and
   Precepts help us to realize equality and patience;
May we undertake the great vows with humility
   and gratitude.

Glossary

anuttara-samyak-sambodhi. A Sanskrit term meaning "complete, unexcelled enlightenment"; an attribute of all Buddhas.

Avalokitesvara Bodhisattva. The bodhisattva of compassion whose name means "Observing the Sounds of the World." He is known as one of the great bodhisattvas of Mahayana Buddhism and is very popular throughout China.

bodhisattva. While the term can describe a practitioner anywhere on the path to Buddhahood, it usually refers to a class of beings who stand on the very edge of full enlightenment but remain in the world to help other beings become enlightened.

Buddha. A Sanskrit word meaning "Awakened One." Though there are many Buddhas, the term typically refers to Sakyamuni Buddha, the historical Buddha and founder of Buddhism. Buddhahood is the attainment and expression that characterizes a Buddha and the ultimate goal of all sentient beings.

Dharma. A Sanskrit word meaning "truth"; referring to the Buddha's teachings, as well as the truth of the universe.

When capitalized, it denotes both the ultimate truth and the teachings of the Buddha. When the term appears in lowercase, it refers to anything that can be thought of, experienced, or named; this usage is close in meaning to the concept of "phenomena."

emptiness. The concept that everything in the world arises due to dependent origination and has no permanent self or substance. All phenomena are said to be empty of an inherently independent self.

enlightenment. The state of awakening to the ultimate truth. This is freedom from all afflictions and suffering.

five aggregates. The five aggregates make up a human being. They are: form, feeling, perception, mental formations, and consciousness.

merit. Blessings that occur because of wholesome deeds.

nirvana. A state of perfect tranquility that is the ultimate goal of Buddhist practice. The original meaning of this word is "extinguished," "calmed," "quieted," "tamed," or "dead." In Buddhism, it refers to the absolute extinction of individual existence or the extinction of all afflictions and desires; it is the state of liberation beyond the cycle of birth and death.

paramita. A Sanskrit word meaning "crossed over" or "perfection." This denotes passage to the other shore of the tranquility of nirvana. This is spiritual success.

prajna. A Sanskrit word meaning "wisdom." This typically refers to a transcendent variety of wisdom that comes from seeing the true nature of reality. Prajna wisdom is considered the highest form of wisdom, the wisdom of insight into the true nature of all phenomena.

Saha World. Saha literally means "endurance." It indicates the present world where we reside, which is full of suffering to be endured. The beings in this world endure suffering and afflictions due to their greed, anger, hatred, and ignorance. Also referred to as "samsara," or the cycle of birth and death. When sentient beings die, they are reborn into one of the six realms of existence: heaven, human, asura, animal, hungry ghost, and hell. The cycle continues as a result of one's karmic actions. Outside of the Saha World exist four additional realms: that of the sravaka, pratekyabuddha, bodhisattva, and Buddha. Taken together with the six realms previously mentioned, they are called the ten realms.

Sakyamuni Buddha. Siddhartha Gautama of the Sakya clan, the historical Buddha and founder of the religion known today as Buddhism. The name "Sakyamuni" means "Sage of the Sakyans." He was born the prince of Kapilavastu, son of King Suddhodana. At the age of twenty-nine, he left the royal palace and his family in search of the meaning of existence. At the age of thirty-five, he attained enlightenment under the bodhi tree. He then spent the next forty-five years expounding his teachings, which include the Four Noble Truths, the Noble Eightfold Path, the law of cause and effect, and dependent origination. At the age of eighty, he entered the state of parinirvana.

Sariputra. One of the ten great disciples of the Buddha. He is known as foremost in wisdom.

sutra. A Sanskrit word used to describe a variety of religious and non-religious writings, but most commonly used in a Buddhist context to refer to the recorded discourses of the Buddha.

Tathagata. One of the ten epithets of a Buddha, literally translated as "Thus Come One," meaning the one who has attained full realization of suchness, which means true essence or actuality. Tathagata is the one dwelling in the absolute, beyond all transitory phenomena, so that he can freely come and go anywhere.

three thousandfold world system. According to Buddhist cosmology, there are an infinite number of worlds. Each world has at its center a Mount Sumeru surrounded by seven oceans with seven rings of golden mountains separating each ocean. Surrounding these are four continents and eight subcontinents. Humans reside on the southern continent of Jambudvipa. When one thousand of these worlds are grouped together it is called a "small world system," one thousand small world systems equal a "medium world system," and one thousand medium world systems equal a "large world system." A "three thousandfold world system" is a combination of these three types of world systems.

World-honored One. One of the ten epithets of the Buddha.

Fo Guang Shan
International Translation Center

Fo Guang Shan International Translation Center is dedicated to translating and distributing quality translations of classical Buddhist texts as well as works by contemporary Buddhist teachers and scholars. We embrace Humanistic Buddhism, and promote Buddhist writing which is accessible, community-oriented, and relevant to daily life. On FGSITC.org you can browse all of our publications, read them online and even download them for FREE, as well as requesting printed copies for you or your organization.

Donors

1000 copies	Jia Peir Wang & Yueh Chin Hsu Wang
500 copies	佛立門文教中心信眾
333 copies	陳淑鈴
200 copies	香港佛光道場、Wei Zhou
167 copies	許麗娟、柯綏
150 copies	佛州奧蘭多分會西區
137 copies	佛光山光明寺
100 copies	佛光山香雲寺、澳洲南天寺、心保和尚、魏梁愛珍、林鶯明、張馨文、黃婕妮、廖家迎、廖樹蘭、陳詩宜、陳麗璧、蔡月珍、蔡素芬、李佩欣合家、Vic Wu & Chu Wu
90 copies	Esther Man
83 copies	林周秀子、高秀珍
67 copies	林麗玉
50 copies	北卡佛光山、關島佛光山、愛民頓講堂、永康法師、覺觀法師、留許秀瓊、孔美蓉、王蓓瑜、史雪美、吳偉康、江素麗、林明彥、林明霏、林猷美、留婉婉、張胡對、張樑溪、曹思蕾、曹啓順、曹維鵬、劉美杏、

劉珀秀、陳力昌、陳騁英、賴沛銘、應美蓮、蔡佳穎、鄭美玲、薛文媛、關許彥、伍碧蓮合家、祝元玲合家、奧克蘭佛光寺信眾、國際佛光會羅蘭分會、佛州奧蘭多分會東區、Wei H. Chang

42 copies　周光奎、施美惹

40 copies　陳東華、陳茂記、張賞、Adam Penn Chen, Anna Chen

35 copies　永印法師、黃玉招、Yuling Yu

33 copies　何敏鈴、劉榕合家

30 copies　慧浩法師、王文姬、王雲嬌、文紹治、朱德秀、何典倫、洪碧雲、黃抽拆、郭倚龍、潘廣涉、譚慧君、羅亞朝、彭民祥合家、Hudson Liu, Serene Liu, Bruce Zhou

28 copies　王徐秀鷥、王偲珊、王筱霞

27 copies　西來寺助念組

26 copies　覺詠法師

25 copies　王洪麗華、阮李純錦、王介強、王亦基、王珮琪、吳寶通、李承岡、李貞儀、林永和、林玉梅、張文儀、張淑美、梁偉還、阮添發、蔡新玉、馬眞、馬金蘭合家、鄂魏靜容合家、Louvenia Ortega, J. G. Custom Tile, Inc.

22 copies　蔡雪鈺

21 copies　黃嬎湉、黃雋琇、黃練石、蔡香蘭

20 copies　有仁法師、吳葉珠月、李鄭巧眞、宋張玫麗、紀江美津、楊周佩秋、方碧玉、方達強、王宗信、王雲嬌、丘英明、

丘英德、丘英龍、吳國賢、吳碧雲、吳錦鑾、何佩芝、
李文惠、林靜珍、房金洲、紀智耀、柯森子、柯慧發、
洪全敏、洪應輝、徐綉琴、高靜瀟、許俊卿、張涵苗、
張筑婷、張翔楷、張瓊華、梁定柱、梁定嫻、梁靖敏、
麥子清、麥亦芃、黃忠仁、單雲秀、曾鈺軒、曾國雄、
楊呂銀、楊海平、楊寒梅、楊雅鈞、楊適豪、莊茗蕎、
趙庭庭、趙庭懿、趙慈蓮、趙興望、廖敏吟、廖朝平、
廖莉薇、甄亮恆、郭瓗儀、陳文英、陳立眞、陳妙洪、
陳素梅、陳惜珍、陳順餘、陳慧娟、陳憲美、陳寶桂、
陳瓊姬、潘綺華、陸美玉、顏淑媛、鄧寶珠、羅鳳娥、
蘇政允、蘇政輔、楊恕、令惜美合家、江寶玲合家、
曾紀濤合家、佛州航太分會、Sunny, Tommy Hsu,
Samson Huang, Cindy Lin, Cailin Liu, Chia Lin Liu,
Lisa Sam, Linda Skybrock, Yu-Lin Sung, Paul Wolf,
Alan Yang, Lereve Skin Institute Inc.

18 copies   林凱俊

17 copies   周湯海倫、吳小虹、周靖妍、馬麗娟、梁蓮鳳、黃氏仙、
黃寶霖、盛阿好、喬于修、喬宣時、湯穎筠、湯穎聰、
賈正文、劉綺雯、劉麗雲、郭雯玲、郭錫湖、陳嘉嘉、
盧漢光、鍾廷昭、鍾秀娜、鍾松杉、鍾紹康、鍾敏霞、
Polly W. S. Chiu, Wai Ho Chiu, Maggie Wong, Randy Wong

16 copies   妙坤法師、陳美珠、班紅、梵悟、佛州天帕分會

15 copies   賴黃碧蓮、卜慧芳、李元穌、李璧妤、黃皓明、
陳金蓮、賴蓆臻、應冬有、應仲婷、應仲傑、羅秀鳳、
蘇朝群、十方大眾

13 copies   黃郭明珠、王喬榮、李碧琴、林顯勳、黃建宏、
黃琦瑛、黃聰樑、趙韋珊、趙偉豪、黎淑和、
Lawrence Lin, Philip Lin

12 copies　曲立正、吳進賢、姚新德、姚繼程、姚繼雄、陳世恩、陳佳億、陳春安、陳柏亭、陳隆志、龍亭廷、蔡佩芬、覺睿

11 copies　畢可坤、屠維愛、楊斌龍、鄭麗卿

10 copies　心昇法師、心勤法師、心馨法師、宏善法師、依宏法師、知德法師、滿光法師、覺凡法師、覺多法師、覺法法師、覺聖法師、覺謙法師、慧靖法師、王陳松花、古黎珊雲、朱張美香、朱劉秋燕、任郭招妹、吳邱街市、李林美琴、余伍小珍、余譚娟玝、施林富美、夏岳迺文、高張文妹、梁民里道、崔李秀蘭、傅洪秀鳳、植村嘉奈、齊黃秋玉、劉羅錦蘭、陳洪秋惠、蔣嚴培珍、蔡胡紅素、蔡邱富美、蕭溫翠美、刁偉汶、刁傳忠、刁潔怡、方蕙蓮、方黎菁、王氏娟、王代鳳、王佩蘭、王美清、王建華、王書先、王書華、王笑歡、王淑玲、王盛蕙、王頌婷、王頌華、王翠薇、王儷玲、石翠玉、白志雄、白美伶、白聖勳、丘月來、史氏美、朱天行、朱自立、朱泉華、朱梅珺、朱喬明、朱貴慕、朱樂山、朱樂水、伍雁慈、任智心、任維嫻、吳元萱、吳文職、吳佩芳、吳金諓、吳美雅、吳健穎、吳慧貞、何大亂、何書明、何書鄉、何曉紀、何麗溶、李小兵、李台元、李安心、李宏莉、李佳蓉、李桂鳳、李梅鳳、李惠雲、李雲鳳、李碧榮、李錄詩、杜美華、江洋銘、余昱興、余海生、林六妹、林光琦、林志御、林明珠、林佩雲、林奕君、林英方、林荻蕽、林逸心、林群泰、林群峰、林鳳珠、林增忠、林慧程、林達興、林蟠平、林蟠雅、林麗玉、林麗青、林寶雲、狄仲傑、卓雅芬、周瑞琴、沈友成、沈友良、沈春香、沈茂秀、姚韻怡、姚藹怡、施娃葵、施淑惠、洪友和、馬燕貞、袁惠玲、翁大溪、唐瑞鳴、孫嘉寧、孫德貴、凌淑如、夏韵琛、高楊玉、高銘俊、留平敏、留俊傑、留芳芳、留婉茵、留港財、留煜棋、留聯泰、留薇蒨、許秀暖、許志豪、許志銘、許琮翔、許覲宏、康秀鑫、張于震、張宗明、張芬蘭、張珮香、張婉薇、張淑娟、張淵順、張嘉媛、張銀球、張燕倩、張學惠、胡月珠、

8 copies　慧宣法師、王張素嬌、王傅惠琴、吳陳純純、麥陳淑英、
王桂美、朱淑惠、吳世俊、吳世英、吳小媚、吳小雲、
吳小鳳、吳允民、吳世銘、吳成鳳、吳祖儀、吳祖賢、
吳寶珍、何志鳴、李若珍、李雲鵬、巫麗霞、林緄俊、
許明亮、許致睿、許迎輝、許國滿、張素娟、張雯惠、
麥順興、曹伍梅、曹其寶、彭文紅、甄中元、翟業英、
劉振和、陳白市、陳英壽、鐘秀蘭、嚴嬉琪、譚容、
Michelle Chen, Tyffany Chen, Charles A Johnson,
Chiwei Lin, Yuhsuan Lin, Quynh Ly, Janet Ng

7 copies　丁柳婷、王映之、王怡茜、何天佑、何綺健、李春麗、
林子婷、林子彭、紀鳳逸、劉靜英、陳玉妹、陳琴文、
龍昌傑、龍星名、龍德富、鄭碧華、譚維漢、
Jason Huynh, Jim Ong

6 copies　石榮馨、吳敏伶、李依鴻、余光忠、佟思齊、林木田、
林秀英、林欣穎、林瑞智、祁益菁、孫秀蕙、張白鈺、
張楷珮、黃少玲、黃則棟、黃韻珊、邱女枝、楊英傑、
游秋萍、陳月華、陳玫媛、應太乾、應良謙、應良駿、
應良鴻、應良翼、應明仁、應明聖、應明誠、應莉露、
蔡青樺、蘭仕會、佟濟、陳超、Evan Li, Isabella Li,
Mei Li, Nathan Li, Peter Li, Shing Li, Kaitlyn Quan,
Lanren Quan, Diamond Tong, Wanna Wu, Sean
Peter Yeh

5 copies　心設法師、心詠法師、有度法師、妙寧法師、妙覺法師、
慧無法師、覺慈法師、方酈玉英、李林春霞、李陳秋榮、
冷喻引葆、林鄭秋花、徐張彩萍、胡葛振玉、莊謝綉卿、
董冷觀明、蔣葉領香、簡陳素香、薛魏阿裡、于瑞如、
于靜雯、孔佩儀、方士軒、方綺薇、牛淑華、王乃欣、
王可欣、王冬梅、王世糧、王明世、王林霞、王美玲、
王秋雲、王康宏、王浩軒、王婉玲、王康熙、王珠嬌、
王淑珍、王淑眞、王熙崑、王興玉、王進財、王賴柑、

石明軒、石佳琪、石佩華、甘米月、古家綦、古詠明、古煥倫、朱威泰、
朱珏葶、朱桂蓮、朱鳳儀、朱興進、伍立安、伍立淵、伍永芳、伍佑娜、
伍佑峻、伍東華、牟敦滬、吳佳穎、吳清圖、吳圖南、吳寶琴、李文光、
李文星、李文卿、李心珠、李玉枝、李昇彥、李承勳、李佳潔、李明翰、
李品妤、李品萱、李美玲、李美雲、李國豪、李偉駿、李惠明、李越抗、
李慎茜、李菩提、李萬來、李選國、江慶章、辛性汝、呂志彥、呂秋宏、
呂連英、余昱燊、林士般、林士隆、林正皓、林光佑、林圳亮、林利橙、
林青瓔、林奕宏、林建昭、林素勤、林家綦、林浩然、林嘉婷、林靜如、
林蘭英、金暐峻、金豪峻、周小菲、周艾琳、周明輝、周金龍、周笑晨、
周祖維、周敏兒、周培蘭、周善在、周愉純、周愉絜、沈雅敏、易貫生、
易穎正、易穎奇、明義軒、明義騰、候霽洋、候霽峰、施吾萱、施吾樺、
韋穎詩、韋穎誼、洪燕貞、徐小微、徐小蓮、徐巧雲、徐笑珍、徐海綦、
徐若蓮、徐荇蔭、徐銀貴、翁嘉君、唐小茹、唐小媚、唐祖勝、孫筱珋、
倪嘉言、夏岳芝、高仁捷、高玉娟、高仕捷、高本傑、高爲宜、高雯雯、
高淑嫻、許東月、許祐溱、許淑梅、許竣理、許耀卿、張玉清、張有容、
張良治、張佑寧、張佳宏、張祖華、張國深、張善月、張凱閔、張喜清、
張程森、張詩卉、張詠欣、張詠儀、張瑜庭、張瑞惠、張錦瑜、張鴻銘、
張麗琴、張馨匀、張耀輝、苗蘊華、梁永恒、梁偉成、梁雪梅、梁媛梅、
梁惜福、梁慧雯、梁慧賢、梁陳雪、胡厚莊、胡榮哲、胡榮顯、章德新、
崔秀珠、強瑞香、黃子榮、黃子睿、黃玉佩、黃朱香、黃秀娟、黃宥榛、
黃柏豪、黃春霖、黃恩庭、黃純毓、黃迎春、黃彩鳳、黃裕仁、黃嘉新、
黃維德、黃穎卿、黃諮華、黃澆聰、黃麗珊、黃寶雲、黃繡葭、邱秀蘭、
彭馨儀、馮少芳、曾宥澄、曾雅慧、曾慧敏、程淑梅、程揚洋、程寧君、
楊綺霞、雷海源、游秋桂、詹達娀、詹勳崇、莊煥章、趙崇尚、趙崇華、
趙嘉慶、廖志珩、管翊里、管邦翔、逢君瑋、逢冠倫、逢麒鈞、劉子安、
劉子愛、劉子筠、劉明倫、劉芳娥、劉玲玲、葉佐勝、葉玫玉、葛振芳、
郭大維、郭卉芝、郭婷婷、郭滿足、歐柏杉、歐凱庭、陳三妹、陳文斌、
陳月燕、陳世華、陳兆洪、陳伯淯、陳明正、陳佩珊、陳東海、陳昌碩、
陳禹丞、陳美美、陳美玲、陳柏愷、陳敏雄、陳國榮、陳超子、陳淑惠、
陳意馨、陳瑞玲、陳嘉雯、陳嘉駿、陳瑞鵬、陳德輝、陳燕香、陳學海、
陳學琴、陳麗貞、陳麗玲、陳寶治、陳譽文、霍沁怡、陸美珍、賴文勝、
賴惟悅、韓筱葉、鍾秀瓊、謝心覺、謝錫來、鄒隆平、蔡文佩、蔡文欣、
蔡文凱、蔡昌佑、蔡承哲、蔡承邦、蔡彥盈、蔡柳娟、蔡緯航、蔡麗華、
戴振華、顏水山、顏鴻恩、魏湘雲、鄭玉美、鄭志忠、鄭志勇、鄭成偉、

鄭俊嬋、鄭創佳、鄭淑芳、鄭碧玉、譚清石、薛崑松、蕭立卿、蕭伊廷、蕭宏欣、鐘瑞芳、蘇玉秀、蘇家穎、蘇碧珊、蘇進和、甘瑞、李琴、李峰、杜宇、呂妙、林桐、常怡、章典、章錦、崔音、葛磊、陳蜜、鄧超、鄧詩、盧克、三寶弟子、Beson 梁、Alexis, Farouk Ahmad, Christchin Beuman, Quoc Binh, Adam J. Brown, Amy E. Brown, Floyd J. Brown, Lisa Chan, Annie Chang, Eric Chang, Nathan A. Chao, Vincent A. Chao, Jason Chau, Chiu Yuen Chen, Lucy Chen, Nancy Chen, Peiyu Chen, Jennifer Cheung, Brian Chu, Clarence Chu, Chris Day, Julia Day, Danny Huang, Kevin Huang, Michelle Huang, Steven Huang, Shuan Mei Kato, David Ke, Eva Ke, Robert Ke, Isaac Khan, Omar Khan, Alexander Kuo, Andrew Kuo, Olivia Kuo, Tony Kuo, Anna Lam, Summer Lam, Tony Lam, Karen Lee, Peter Lee, Emily Li, Ester S Moreno, Avery Mytych, Eleanor Mytych, Michael O'Neill, Jazmine Osier, Maxwell Osier, Natale Panzeca, Bao Phuc, Miaowei Shih, Joanne Tanyongkul, Yijin Wang, Ken Woo, Annie Wu

4 copies　歐陽秋月、陳蔡素珠、王喬雲、朱泳雯、朱俊燃、伊凡諾、吳芷欣、吳芷洋、吳錦一、吳錦濤、何蜀圖、李孟橋、李慧敏、李慧清、李麗珠、周敏飛、高志昆、張文芳、張文嘉、曾卓瑜、楊若卿、楊達志、游子珮、游尹姿、游祥人、劉淑華、劉靜芝、陳玉燕、陳嘉惠、陳嘉儀、陳蘭嬌、鄒德順、蔡嘉禾、蔡璧駿、鄭佩珍、鄭涵文、鄭碧月、鄭榕欽、鄧秀蘭、王璃、李佳、李曜、邵雪、國陞工程企業有限公司、May Hui, Tat Yuen Lau, Ha Thi Vo, Siu Hung Yee

3 copies　覺是法師、林陳雲香、胡林淑貞、黃許蘭卿、王少靜、王梓鍵、王梓權、王國耀、王淑薇、王敬思、王敬浩、王敬雅、王榮華、王夢蘭、王麗燕、朱洪帥、朱陳清、

吳卓泳、吳美英、吳泳璇、吳敏慧、何祥鈺、何綺蘭、
何靜婉、李可晴、李玉華、李良竹、李思彤、李敏欣、
李浩威、李捷萍、李瑞屏、李德淳、林香玉、林風宏、
林吳信、林端源、林慧玲、林慧雯、林慧萍、周英奇、
周培垚、周添壽、周慶雲、周麗眞、施品君、韋宇清、
洪秋月、徐德坤、徐劍雄、唐修敏、唐修華、孫英玄、
孫梅雪、許宗正、張惠美、胡月芬、胡錫位、畢寶方、
畢寶如、黃小英、黃有泉、黃金玉、黃東源、黃建平、
黃炳年、黃美花、黃柏鈞、黃柏閎、黃淑惠、黃詩友、
黃麗芳、傅瀚鈺、楊昌能、楊昌陵、楊祉寧、楊凱勛、
詹玉女、詹翊宏、趙建軍、趙珈祺、廖玉如、劉靜炎、
葉一帆、葉青樹、葉衍冰、葉莉青、葉莉莉、葛思琦、
郭德宇、郭德宙、郭德城、陳志華、陳昀佐、陳昀佑、
陳怡安、陳冠良、陳芳如、陳芳純、陳紫絢、陳勝政、
陳淑娥、陳榮斌、陳潘雪、陳關生、駱彩群、謝文郡、
謝啓泉、謝瑩慧、鄒佑民、鄒慶宜、鄒慶頡、蔡書琪、
簡振龍、鄭曼枝、鄧彩燕、羅靖宜、蘇文鴻、蘇彥嘉、
蘇祖瑞、蘇家華、蘇家齡、蘇宸瀚、蘇國才、蘇鈺之、
文來、朱越、朱琳、胡禾、黃林、黃傑、劉葦、劉戀、
葉英、葉楠、郭珈、陳思、顏錦、三寶弟子、
Evelyne, Ismael Alonso, Keith Bassett, Richelle Charisse,
Richie Clarence, Melinsa Cho, Caroline Chou, Krystal
Harris, Felix Huang, Jason Huang, Lydia Huang,
Ashley Kang, Tae Sun Kang, Thio Troeng Khian,
Kloe Sin Kim, Joshua Doangou Lee, Tiffany Jinsan Lee,
Wen Lin, Tanya Scalfe, Isabella Sun, Katherine Sun,
Donny Tu, Jolie Tu, Michael Tu, W. A. Vancuylenburg,
Peggy Wilkinson, Merianny Wiryo, Kit Sum Wong,
Raymond Wu, Cabot Yu, Betty Yuen, Herrison Zhao,
Yu Zhen

2 copies　心清法師、如緣法師、歐陽慶曉、劉陳桂妹、葉林素梅、
陳李玉雙、謝黃惠玲、王彥勛、王彥智、王曉筱、
王肇隆、文錦泉、石億智、石億雄、石穆祥、朱余好、

朱延文、朱詠儀、任義宇、任煒薇、吳坤霖、吳惠芳、何玉英、何秀媚、
何敏儀、何富文、何靜宜、李小娜、李中良、李友成、李月琛、李玉專、
李向榮、李佩珍、李弦達、李欣潔、李家助、李振華、李國卿、李智英、
李琪琪、李鳳梨、李樂柔、李樂銘、李諾恆、宋曼妹、江民龍、江秉樺、
江柳馮、江莉蘋、江懿文、江驛恩、余相玲、林于韻、林玉貴、林玉葉、
林秀春、林秋霞、林勝雄、林寶蘭、周康寧、沈永仁、武昕曈、姜瑩瑩、
姚玉婷、姚懿貞、施喜心、施雅珍、施藝敏、柯炯炯、柯彬彬、柯愛士、
柯繼雄、洪雪瓊、洪欽霖、徐玉英、徐松貞、容鎮南、許世傑、許秀瓊、
許燕玲、張文寧、張全勝、張合梅、張因覺、張再齡、張秋月、張嘉慶、
梁小杏、梁沁淼、梁鈺銘、梁麗娥、崔小玲、崔廣興、區惠意、黃永成、
黃建鎮、黃思瑩、黃柏維、黃㛃菊、黃渝雯、黃焯楠、黃琬珊、黃鈺淳、
黃達莊、黃衛權、黃韻眞、黃麒麟、彭衍圖、彭衍端、馮年利、馮恆花、
馮恆健、曾尹澍、曾尹璿、曾永成、楊丁燕、楊九仔、楊天智、楊建國、
楊堅浩、楊堅得、楊堅頴、楊清榮、楊劍萍、莊千瑢、廖叔敏、溫寶瑩、
連麗珠、連麗卿、甄杏嬋、劉少玉、劉月淑、劉四妹、劉玉蘭、劉有勝、
劉見屏、劉珍珍、劉桂芳、劉琇瑩、劉福明、劉耀智、劉覲娣、葉凡瑄、
葉玉燕、葉世安、葉國權、葉勝倫、談家耀、郭人溢、郭价祐、歐婉芬、
陳正倫、陳白珊、陳白純、陳利貴、陳俊傑、陳柏合、陳悦恩、陳英傑、
陳泰宇、陳泰儒、陳素萍、陳國濱、陳國灝、陳婉珊、陳婉瑛、陳梅嬌、
陳梓焌、陳梓謙、陳景曾、陳靖瑩、陳碧香、陳嘉琳、陳慶華、陳潔英、
陳輝群、陳憶文、陳賽妹、陳麗梅、潘宣文、潘俐伶、潘健民、賴弘力、
鍾錦星、蔡如春、蔡秀炎、蔡佩伻、蔡侑軒、蔡美萱、蔡超凡、蔡礎蔓、
蔡礎蔚、蔡礎騏、蔡禮騏、蔡馥駿、簡士傑、簡士翔、魏碧香、鄭里其、
鄭開明、鄧家俊、鄧家傑、鄧浩然、薛文智、薛世瑞、薛芳玲、蕭玉英、
鐘政倫、羅蘭根、顧仁語、顧仁曦、顧芝庭、顧植明、何璐、
余軼、肖虹、張妹、楊瓊、劉增、郭金、陳妹、陳曦、鍾靈、
Chace Arnold, Anli Chen, Ching Ching Chen, Yin Chin Choo,
Christopher Fang, Kaitlyn Fang, Gregor Grant, Rosemary Grant,
Cina Hung, Raja Kumar, Panny Lu, Bianca Ng, Byron Ng, Jebas-
tian Ritter, Bertha Ross, Gregory Ross, Amy Tay, Robert Tcheng,
Jenny Vong, Phillip Vong, Wilson Vong, Hudson Wong, Julie
Wong, Carol Yi Yu Zhang

1 copy　　　心由法師、心宙法師、心菩法師、有承法師、有容法師、

田沺實香、田煙實香、吳楊秀蓮、李廖賢妹、林呂香妹、俞柯桂妹、
許郭千瑜、梁施英英、胡許寶珠、曾黃秋玉、莊陳玲玉、廖許軟樣、
劉呂金香、葉羅菊蘭、董李金蘭、陳林金梅、陳黎帶妹、陳陸穎慈、
陳鄭美女、謝裴月雲、鄭李淑敏、鄭呂碧蓮、藍林桂朱、藍黃雪貞、
藍曹念深、丁玉基、丁寶妹、方門焯、王中榮、王金枝、王秀萍、王珍鈺、
王韋鈞、王彩繁、王然峰、王義秀、王嘉祥、王維中、王燕玲、文近容、
文運輝、尹淑芳、甘佩儒、田雁翎、田麗明、史含泓、史美璞、史習垚、
史習瑾、朱玥兒、朱彩明、朱國輝、朱瑞嵐、朱劍輝、朱燊輝、全瓊蘭、
任明駿、任達朗、任燦峰、仲維虹、吳旻祐、吳佩珊、吳固崇、吳岳聲、
吳承軒、吳承駿、吳松聲、吳冠諒、吳施梅、吳美慧、吳家助、吳振淵、
吳素娟、吳素慧、吳崇誠、吳章返、吳進旭、吳懿樺、何佩娟、李小白、
李元生、李月華、李王過、李仲強、李因翰、李志海、李志偉、李志豪、
李佳諭、李佳運、李孟榛、李宜婕、李岳陵、李弦澤、李明怡、李欣芝、
李品呈、李品萱、李昱徵、李姿嫻、李威德、李威儒、李家成、李家忻、
李家承、李家興、李妍枝、李淑貞、李淑芬、李淑淨、李淑慧、李貴萍、
李傅賢、李照子、李傳明、李義明、李慶宗、李嬋娟、李翰林、李曉雨、
李曉燕、李陳做、李蓮蓮、李澤棠、李瀚恩、江孟倫、江連枚、呂永裕、
呂冬領、呂東榮、呂美慧、呂娉婷、呂敦漢、林大珍、林日晨、林世炎、
林再華、林坤仲、林欣啓、林君綺、林佳瑩、林宗禮、林勇如、林品妤、
林美津、林美雲、林禹賢、林庭蕓、林敏兒、林敏春、林得輝、林雅宜、
林靖恩、林鳳珠、林鳳梅、林曉賓、周世浩、周件文、周俊傑、周美玲、
周穎思、周穎琪、周總富、沈月香、沈永鑫、沈茱堅、沈宥卉、沈宥丞、
沈春香、沈綺芸、沈麗鳳、姚少雯、姚滿德、候美開、施逸柔、施珵濬、
施順騰、柯安隆、柯佩吟、柯順堯、柯琳紫、柯憲宏、封志明、洪志珮、
洪偉鳴、洪舜文、徐桂芳、徐興維、徐潔好、倪一鳴、倪劍萍、倪飄萍、
高玉瓔、高江蓮、高承業、高華隆、秦偉平、秦曉蕾、芮楚基、許正揚、
許宏任、許志宇、許秀鳳、許金碤、許宥騫、許晏碩、許淳雅、許鈞彥、
許裕昇、許維君、許靜彤、許鍾岳、張安喬、張式萱、張秀梓、張秀陶、
張柚子、張勁梅、張美鳳、張剩勇、張雁翔、張筱惠、張慧珠、張曉慧、
張麗珠、張繼紅、梁考昌、梁君豪、梁荔紅、梁晉誠、梁善祺、梁達智、
梁智堅、梁智熹、梁翠玲、梁慧美、梁錦榮、梁潔玲、梁禮祺、梁艷玲、
胡月娥、胡孝芳、胡孝菽、胡建國、胡惠芳、胡慧君、胡鴻藩、胡麗純、
麥煥彩、麥曉春、曹恩郡、曹晏郡、浦合女、黃士娟、黃月雲、黃玉涵、
黃自豪、黃色陽、黃宣婕、黃宣穎、黃春梅、黃美蓮、黃栢健、黃國楳、

黃素穎、黃淑娟、黃清淯、黃淑鈴、黃景湖、黃義倫、黃義凱、黃資宥、
黃頌稀、黃慧昌、黃蕭英、黃麗敏、黃麗鳳、喻美玲、邱文立、邱文業、
邱勝娥、邱靖茜、彭秀娟、彭員淑、馮宇雋、馮福安、馮愛玲、馮綺文、
馮麗茹、曾可瑩、曾美華、曾炳輝、曾祝嬋、曾素香、曾婉嬋、曾輝元、
曾新發、程愛華、楊士青、楊伊三、楊育荙、楊承翰、楊淨婷、楊培銓、
楊華彬、楊樂如、雷琪玫、湯先清、湯有榮、湯宛蓉、湯俊賢、湯國鈞、
湯愛嵐、詹百合、詹浩傑、莊永韶、莊名英、莊秋媛、莊竣安、莊鳳仁、
莊曜庭、莊曜豪、趙文生、趙若廣、趙美蘭、趙愛花、溫心薇、溫御雅、
裴冠博、劉光國、劉克成、劉冠孝、劉洋宏、劉秋君、劉秋妤、劉美芬、
劉亮稼、劉容伯、劉國順、劉惠玲、劉湅豐、劉綺梅、劉銘裕、劉慧美、
劉衛傑、劉穎安、劉穎嘉、劉寶儀、葉天士、葉彥浩、葉俊傑、葉普門、
葉群娣、葉慈德、葉錦楑、葉澤瀅、董松峯、董學儒、黎思敏、黎海晴、
黎偉雄、黎嘉敏、黎耀祥、郭世宗、郭宇桓、郭松竹、郭彥均、郭冠萱、
郭富田、郭業聲、郭簡粉、陳文雄、陳民生、陳伊娜、陳志行、陳志傑、
陳秀琴、陳沚興、陳佳正、陳佳圓、陳怡宙、陳來源、陳亭因、陳亭而、
陳奕如、陳衍崧、陳昱儒、陳柏臻、陳亮競、陳倩弘、陳素美、陳書晴、
陳逢源、陳國棟、陳崎曜、陳崇曜、陳惠明、陳惠芳、陳惠蓉、陳富隆、
陳琮崴、陳紫楊、陳紫源、陳雲瑩、陳湘穎、陳雅歷、陳雅麟、陳敬華、
陳瑋翔、陳瑞新、陳瑞瑜、陳頌霖、陳幗貞、陳幗琴、陳嘉儀、陳鳳嬌、
陳銘霖、陳樹波、陳龍英、陳鎮江、陳麗雅、盧洪威、盧劍兒、盧劍芬、
盧劍貞、盧劍紫、潘嬡欄、錢俊達、錢信諺、錢虹樺、錢偉明、賴芳美、
蔣俊仁、蔣美珊、鍾建萍、鍾夢倩、謝吉萍、郗永康、郗皓瑋、郗祺靜、
郗瑄琳、蔡秀彩、蔡美華、蔡淑貞、蔡雪梅、蔡藍顏、繆彬彬、繆智純、
繆智輝、繆智賢、繆業祥、繆銳漢、顏大欽、顏志成、顏瑞瑩、轟亦成、
簡柏垚、簡燁軒、魏妤恩、魏辰翰、鄭少川、鄭少山、鄭春霖、鄭清朝、
鄭凱隆、鄭凱邁、鄭筱沅、鄭鳳婷、鄭鳳嘉、鄭鳳齡、鄭繩針、鄭麗芳、
鄭麗明、鄧家明、鄧桔章、鄧素銘、鄧偉宏、鄧偉源、鄧偉麟、鄧啓偉、
鄧碧華、鄧樂希、譚宏如、譚梓朗、譚曉柔、薛人凱、薛武洮、薛傑登、
薛雅齡、關嘉龍、關燕萍、鐘淑珍、藍承青、藍美青、藍章華、藍彗禎、
藍鈞豪、藍雯瀞、藍增青、騰京民、蘇天裕、龔俊誠、龔建國、龔艷青、
牛牛、王歡、文風、何燕、李勇、李茵、李彬、李慧、林澄、林麒、林鑫、
倪炎、張風、馮好、馮桂、楊薇、葉毅、陳昕、陳奕、鍾勤、蔡月、魏衛、
龔偉、自強 Routier, 自恩 Routier, Nicole 梁, Cooper 黃, Michelle 黃,
Charlie Bove, Eddie G. Brackin, Zina Bui, Daniel Chan, Amanda

Chang, Siu King Cheng, Tina Chin, Gloria Chiu, Barbara Cruz, Joseph P Desantis, Ian Fatherley, Verin Fatherley, Gabriel Forte, Vincent Giuliani, Betty Rusmiaty Halim, Aaron Rhys Hewitt, Connor Dale Hewitt, Thi Xuong Huynh, Anthony Jim, Kathy Jim, Theresa Jim, David James Knight, Ashwin Kumar, Naveen Kumar, Kim Chi Huynh Le, Cherrie Luu, Jimmy Luu, Kathleen Luu, Ryan Luu, Ben Mai, Eric Mai, David Morin, Noah Lee Morin, Timothy Moy, Diem Quynh Le Nguyen, Leon Nhat Nguyen, Alexanser Mukarsi Pangestu, Angelina Pangestu, Melissa Francesca Pangestu, Michelle Stephanie Pangestu, Robert Sansjaja Pangestu, Kingstan Saw, Winstan Saw, Teh Si, Jonathan E Smyth, Opal Smyth, Soonhee Smyth, Wing Yun Suen, Arthur Tsaknias, Natalie Tsui, Rong Tsui, Warren Tsui, Kenneth Wade, Tiffany Wade, Alan Wong, Myradel Zamora, Leon Zhou, Lily Zhou

Thank you to all who donated to support the printing and distribution of this booklet.